EFFECTIVE
PRESENTATION
SKILLS

EFFECTIVE PRESENTATION SKILLS

Steve Mandel

KOGAN
PAGE

First published in the United States of America
in 1987 by Crisp Publications Inc, 95 First Street,
Los Altos, California 94022, USA

This edition first published in Great Britain in 1988
by Kogan Page Ltd, 120 Pentonville Road, London N1 9JN

Reprinted 1988, 1989, 1990, 1991, 1992, 1994, 1995

British Library Cataloguing in Publication Data

Mandel, Steve
  Effective presentation skills: a practical
  guide for better speaking.
  1. Public speaking
  I. Title
  808.5'1   PN4121

  ISBN 1-85091-554-7
  ISBN 1-85091-555-5 Pbk

Typeset by DP Photosetting, Aylesbury, Bucks
Printed and bound in Great Britain by
Clays Ltd, St Ives plc

Contents

Preface   7

To the Reader   9

Definitions   10

1. Assess Your Skills   11

2. Dealing with Anxiety   17

3. Planning the Presentation   23

4. Organising Your Presentation   27

5. Developing and Using Visual Aids   37

6. Preparing for Your Presentation   53

7. Delivering the Presentation   59

Final Review Checklist   69

Further Reading from Kogan Page   73

Preface

The study of how to give effective speeches dates back to ancient Greece. Around 350 BC Aristotle wrote his famous *Rhetoric*, now considered to be one of the first formal books on the subject. Now, 2300 years later, we are still struggling with the same problems the Greeks encountered and that speakers have struggled with throughout the ages.

The advent of technology has both complicated and simplified the task of the speaker. For example, today it is possible to produce complex graphs on a computer that will, in turn, produce overhead transparencies. But how much information should we put on that graph? And, most important, where does that graph fit into the organisational plan (if there is one) of the speech?

Effective Presentation Skills attempts to answer the fundamental questions of how to prepare and deliver an effective speech. Proven techniques are presented that will give a reader the necessary skills to give more confident, enthusiastic and persuasive presentations. Topics such as: how to use body language effectively; how to organise thoughts and information for maximum impact; how to develop and use visual aids, as well as (of course) how to deliver what you have prepared.

This book provides some theory but more often presents simple and practical suggestions on how to give more effective presentations.

To the Reader

There is a myth that great speakers are born not made, that somehow certain individuals have the innate ability to stand in front of an audience without a sign of nervousness, and give a moving, dynamic speech. Well, that just isn't so!

People we consider great speakers have usually spent years developing and practising their skill. They had to start at the beginning and learn the basics of organisation, preparation, delivery and overcoming their nerves. Once they had mastered the basics, they continued to build upon their abilities.

Professional athletes practise constantly because they know that otherwise they will not survive. To an outsider, the thought of a professional golfer (for example) spending hour upon hour practising the basics may seem ridiculous. But to that professional, the mastery of those basic skills is the very foundation of success.

Learning to be a better speaker is similar to learning any activity. In the beginning it can be frustrating. After a few lessons where you learn some theory and practise some of the basic skills, things usually improve. Learning to do anything well takes constant practice and a mastery of the basics.

Speaking is no different. Before becoming comfortable as a speaker you need to learn some basic skills and then actively seek places to practise them. This may mean taking every opportunity to speak in an organised setting. The more experience you gain, the more proficient and comfortable you will become.

Steve Mandel

Definitions

The terms 'speech' and 'presentation' are often used interchangeably. For our purposes it is useful to understand the difference.

A presentation is a type of speech. Typically, when we think of a speech we think of a dedication speech, a political speech, a speech of tribute or some similar event that is more public in nature than a presentation would be.

Presentations are speeches that are usually given in a business, technical, professional or scientific environment. The audience is likely to be more specialised than those attending a typical speech event.

Although the difference between speeches and presentations is slight, this book leans towards helping those who give presentations. But, because a presentation is a type of speech, there are ideas and skills in this book that will also be helpful to any speech-maker.

CHAPTER 1
Assess Your Skills

Evaluate yourself

Tick the category that best describes you as a speaker.

Category	Characteristics
_____ *Avoider*	An avoider does everything possible to escape from having to stand in front of an audience. In some cases avoiders may seek careers that do not involve making presentations.
_____ *Resister*	A resister is scared of speaking in public. Resisters may not be able to avoid speaking as part of their job, but they never encourage it. When they do speak they do so painfully and with great reluctance.
_____ *Accepter*	The accepter will give presentations as part of the job but doesn't seek opportunities to do so. Accepters occasionally give a presentation and feel as though they did a good job. They even find that once in a while they are quite persuasive, and enjoy speaking in front of a group.

_____ *Seeker*   A seeker looks for opportunities to speak. The seeker understands that anxiety can be a stimulant which fuels enthusiasm during a presentation. Seekers work at building their professional communication skills and self-confidence by speaking often.

Evaluate your current presentation skills

To be a more effective presenter it is useful to examine your present skills. The following evaluation can help identify the areas on which to focus in order to increase your competence. Please read each statement and circle the number that best describes yourself. Then as you read through the book, concentrate on those items you marked 1, 2 or 3.

	Always				**Never**
1. I identify some basic objectives before planning a presentation.	5	4	3	2	1
2. I analyse the values, needs and limitations of my audience.	5	4	3	2	1
3. I write down some main ideas first, in order to build a presentation around them.	5	4	3	2	1
4. I incorporate both a preview and review of the main ideas.	5	4	3	2	1
5. I develop an introduction that will catch the attention of my audience and still provide the necessary background information.	5	4	3	2	1
6. My conclusion refers back to the introduction and, if appropriate, contains a call-to-action statement.	5	4	3	2	1
7. The visual aids I use are carefully prepared, simple, easy to read, and make an impact.	5	4	3	2	1
8. The number of visual aids will enhance, not detract from, my presentation.	5	4	3	2	1

		Always				Never
9.	If my presentation is persuasive, I support it with logical arguments.	5	4	3	2	1
10.	I use anxiety to fuel the enthusiasm of my presentation, not hold me back.	5	4	3	2	1
11.	I ensure the benefits suggested to my audience are clear and compelling.	5	4	3	2	1
12.	I communicate ideas enthusiastically.	5	4	3	2	1
13.	I rehearse so there is a minimum use of notes and maximum attention paid to my audience.	5	4	3	2	1
14.	My notes contain only 'key words' so I avoid reading from a manuscript.	5	4	3	2	1
15.	My presentations are rehearsed standing up and using visual aids.	5	4	3	2	1
16.	I prepare answers to anticipated questions, and practise replying to them.	5	4	3	2	1
17.	I arrange seating (if appropriate) and check audio-visual equipment in advance of the presentation.	5	4	3	2	1
18.	I maintain good eye contact with the audience at all times.	5	4	3	2	1
19.	My gestures are natural and not restricted by anxiety.	5	4	3	2	1
20.	My voice is strong and clear, and not monotonous.	5	4	3	2	1

Total score _____

If you scored between 80 and 100, you are an accomplished speaker who simply needs to maintain basic skills through practice.

If your total score was between 60 and 80, you have the potential to become a highly effective presenter.

If your score was between 40 and 60, this book can help you significantly.

If you scored between 30 and 40, you should show dramatic improvement with practice.

If your total was below 30, roll up your sleeves and dig in. It may not be easy – but you can make excellent progress if you try.

When you have finished the course, take this evaluation again and compare your scores. You should be pleased with the progress you have made.

Set some goals

If your score on the previous page was:

90–100   You have the qualities of an excellent presenter.

70–89   You are above average but could improve in some areas.

Below 69   This course should help you.

What do you want to achieve?

Using the information from the self-evaluation form on pages 12 and 13, tick those boxes that indicate goals that you would like to achieve.

I hope to:

☐ understand the anxiety I feel before a presentation and learn how to use it constructively.

☐ learn how to organise my thoughts and material in a logical and concise manner.

☐ develop the necessary skills to communicate my ideas enthusiastically, and develop a more dynamic presentation style.

☐ transform question-and-answer sessions into an enjoyable and productive part of the presentation process.

☐ construct visual aids that make an impact, and use them effectively during my presentation.

CHAPTER 2
Dealing With Anxiety

Anxiety is a natural state that arises whenever we are under stress. Giving a presentation will normally cause some stress. When this happens, physiological changes take place that may cause symptoms such as a nervous stomach, sweating, shaking hands and legs, rapid breathing, and/or increased heart rate.

Don't worry! If you have any of these symptoms before or during a presentation you are normal. If none of these things happens you are one in a million. Almost everyone experiences some stress before presentations, even when the task is something simple like, 'tell the group something about yourself'. The trick is to make your excess energy work for you.

If you learn to make stress work for you, it can be the fuel for more enthusiastic and dynamic presentations. The next few pages will teach you how to use your stress positively and help you to become a better presenter.

As someone once said, 'the trick is to get those butterflies in your stomach all to fly in one direction'.

Bill is an engineer with an electronics firm. In two weeks he has to deliver a major presentation to managers from several divisions, on a project he is proposing. He knows his subject, but his audience will be examining his proposal very closely, and Bill is certain he will be asked some very difficult questions. Every time Bill thinks about planning what to say, he gets too nervous to begin work.

If Bill's problem of anxiety before a presentation sounds familiar then the following may help.

Tips for reducing anxiety

1. Organise

Lack of organisation is one of the major causes of anxiety. Later in this book you will learn a simple technique for organising your presentation. Knowing that your thoughts are well organised will give you more confidence, which will allow you to channel your energy into the presentation.

2. Visualise

Imagine walking into a room, being introduced, delivering your presentation with enthusiasm, fielding questions with confidence and leaving the room knowing you did a good job. Mentally rehearse this sequence with all the details of your particular situation, and it will help you to focus on what you need to do to be successful.

3. Practise

Many speakers rehearse a presentation mentally or with just their lips. Instead, you should practise standing up, as if an audience were in front of you, and use your visual aids (if you have them). At least two dress rehearsals are recommended. If possible, have somebody assess the first one for you and/or have it videotaped. Watch the playback, listen to the assessment and incorporate any changes you feel are required before your final practice session. *There is no better preparation than this.*

Carol is an account executive with a software company. She has been asked to present the sales figures for her region at the company's national sales meeting. Her colleague John is finishing his remarks and in two minutes she will have to stand up and make her presentation. She is extremely nervous when she needs to be calm and collected.

Carol's situation is quite common. If you get very nervous immediately before speaking, try some of the following exercises next time you're waiting for your turn to stand up and speak:

4. Breathe deeply
When your muscles tighten and you feel nervous, you may not be breathing deeply enough. The first thing to do is to sit up, erect but relaxed, and inhale deeply a number of times.

5. Relax
Instead of thinking about the tension – relax. As you breathe in, tell yourself, 'I am', and out 'relaxed'. Try to clear your mind of everything except the repetition of the 'I am relaxed' statement and continue this exercise for several minutes.

6. Release tension
As tension increases and your muscles tighten, nervous energy can get locked into the limbs. This unreleased energy may cause your hands and legs to shake. Before standing up to give a presentation, it is a good idea to try to release some of this pent up tension by doing a simple, unobtrusive isometric exercise.

Starting with your toes and calf muscles, tighten your muscles up through your body finally making a fist (ie toes, feet, calves, thighs, stomach, chest, shoulders, arms and fingers). Immediately release all the tension and take a deep breath. Repeat this exercise until you feel the tension start to drain away. Remember, this exercise is to be done quietly so that no one knows you're relaxing!

Andrew is an accountant with a major financial organisation. When he gives presentations he gets very nervous. He sweats, his hands tremble, his voice becomes monotonous (and at times inaudible). He also fidgets and looks at his notes or the overhead projector screen, not at his audience. He can hardly wait to finish and return to his seat.

Andrew's plight is not uncommon. You may not have all these

symptoms but you can probably understand them. The following techniques will help you in situations where you get nervous while speaking.

7. Move around

Speakers who stand in one spot and never gesture become tense. In order to relax you need to release tension by stretching your muscles. If you find you are locking your arms in one position when you speak, then practise releasing them so that they do the same as they would if you were in an animated one-to-one conversation.

Upper body movement is important, but moving with your feet can release tension as well. You should be able to take a few steps, either side-to-side or towards the audience. When speaking from a lectern you can move around the side of it for emphasis (if you have a movable microphone). This movement will help release tension and never fails to draw the audience into the presentation. If you can't move to the side of the lectern, an occasional half-step to one side will help loosen muscular tension.

8. Eye contact with the audience

Try to make your presentation similar to a one-to-one conversation. Treat your audience as individuals. Look at people as you speak. The eye contact should help you relax because you become less isolated from the audience, and react to their interest in you.

Section review:
Dealing with anxiety checklist

Tick those items which you intend to practise and incorporate in future presentations.

I plan to:

- ☐ Organise my material

- ☐ Visualise myself delivering a successful presentation

- ☐ Rehearse by standing up and using all my visual aids

- ☐ Breathe deeply just prior to speaking

- ☐ Relax with simple, unobtrusive isometric techniques

- ☐ Release my tension in a positive way

- ☐ Stay relaxed and natural by moving when I speak

- ☐ Maintain good eye contact with my audience

Practice makes perfect

CHAPTER 3
Planning the Presentation

Part of planning a presentation means that you must ask yourself why, not what. The 'what' part will be answered when you begin to organise your thoughts. In the beginning you should concern yourself with *why* you are giving a presentation to a particular audience. The answer to this question should help you plan your presentation.

For example, you have been asked to give a presentation to a group of managers in your company on next year's departmental budget. Don't start writing down what you expect to say. Instead, ask yourself what you want to accomplish with your presentation. Will you be asking for a budget increase, or presenting a plan showing how you can operate on less money? Think about your specific objectives before preparing your presentation.

Planning your presentation

Can you imagine building a house without a set of plans? Before anyone can build a house, they need plans to guide the purchase of their materials and to show how these materials will be used. In the same way, a plan for your presentation will make the actual work of putting it together much more efficient. A two-tier process – developing objectives and assessing your audience – will help.

Step 1. Develop objectives
The first step is to write down in a simple sentence what your

objective(s) might be. For example: 'My objective is to inform my audience about progress on my research', or, 'My objective is to persuade upper management to grant my department a 20 per cent budget increase.' Business and technical presentations are generally either informative or persuasive. The difference between the two is explained below.

In an informative presentation you are not normally trying to change anyone's behaviour, attitude, or beliefs. You are simply delivering the facts. An example of this type of presentation would be a report in which you simply inform others about progress on a project.

In a persuasive presentation you are trying to change some aspects of your audience's behaviour, attitude or beliefs. For example, you may want them to accept your plans; give you money; change directions on a project etc. The majority of presentations delivered in professional settings are persuasive.

Step 2. Assessing your audience
Put yourself in the shoes of the people who will be listening to your presentation!

When assessing your audience you have three items to consider:

1. *What are the values, needs and constraints on your audience?*
   With smaller groups you can provide more in-depth analysis because you usually know more about the individuals that comprise that group. In larger groups you may have to look at more general ideas.

2. *How well informed is your audience?*
   Have you ever been in a situation where the presenter used abbreviations, acronyms or technical terms that were unfamiliar to the audience? If you have any doubts, it is best to assume that the audience does not understand any specialised terms you might use. If some must be used, explain them briefly.

3. *What will work, what won't work?*
   You need to ask yourself what types of arguments and

evidence will gain the most favourable reaction from the audience. And conversely, what types of arguments and evidence will gain an unfavourable reaction. Then plan your remarks accordingly.

This form should help you plan more efficiently for any presentation.

Audience analysis worksheet

1. My objectives in relation to my audience are:

_____

_____

2. Values that need to be considered with this particular audience include:

_____

_____

3. Special needs of this particular audience:

_____

_____

4. Constraints that must be recognised when speaking to this particular audience.

_____

_____

5. I would rate my audience's knowledge of the topic and technical terminology to be:

   High _____   Low _____   Mixed _____   Unknown _____

6. My assessment of the audience's willingness to accept the ideas I present is:

   High _____   Low _____   Mixed _____   Unknown _____

7. My audience has an opinion of me as a speaker (prior to the presentation) as:

   Good _____ Poor _____ Mixed _____ Unknown _____

8. Examples of supporting ideas and arguments which may work well:

   _____

   _____

9. Examples of supporting ideas and arguments that may cause a negative reaction _____

   _____

CHAPTER 4
Organising Your Presentation

Organising your thoughts

It is always a good idea to start organising the body of the speech and not worry about the introduction until later. Introductions are often generated by what goes into the body. Effective speakers have learned to build from the centre of their speech outwards. Some suggestions that might help you follow:

Step 1. Brainstorm main ideas

Using index cards, brainstorm some possible main ideas for your presentation. Write one idea on each card. Let the ideas flow at this point, don't edit (that will come later). The strategy is to generate as many ideas as possible.

Once you have a large number of ideas, begin eliminating some. Try to end up with between two and five main ideas. This is a typical number for a presentation. If you have more than five ideas you should reduce them by making some of them subpoints.

Example

Suppose you were asked to give a presentation to upper management to defend the need for your department's request for a 20 per cent budget increase next year. You know it is going to be a persuasive presentation, and you have completed your audience analysis sheet (page 25). You created 10 to 15 original

Step 2. State the subpoints

Once you have the main points of your presentation, it is time to develop supporting ideas. These may consist of explanations, data or other evidence to support your main ideas as shown in our example.

Main ideas
(General assertions)

Sub ideas
(Specifics)

Main ideas		
We need to update our computer system	More programmers are needed to develop our systems	We must finance development
Old system is antiquated	Will save £ immediately by creating proprietary programs	Need new data communications system
Can't use latest software	Will be less dependent on outside vendors	New technology allows for better quality at same cost

New personnel will contribute fresh ideas	Can reassign most staff from within company	Old system costs are increasing because of inefficiency
Need new programs	Will help keep us competitive	Many breakdowns recently
New high speed printers will help develop new products	Can develop new products	Hard to replace parts

You may have more or less subpoints in your presentation. Once you have completed this procedure, rearrange your cards to suit your needs. Try different arrangements to see what will work best. Always keep your objectives and audience in mind.

ideas to focus on and have narrowed them down to the following three:

We need to update our computer system	More programmers are needed to develop our systems	We must finance development

These three ideas are the general assertions you plan to make to your audience. Specific explanations, evidence and benefits will become your subpoints.

Step 3. State the benefits

In persuasive presentations it is necessary to tell the audience *specifically* what benefits they will receive if they do what you ask. Benefits can be stated before going into the body of your presentation, or at the end of the body, or ideally, in both places. From the previous example (Why our department needs a 20 per cent larger budget next year) we might summarise the following benefits to our audience:

1. More money in our department will allow for a new computer system that will keep us competitive in our industry.
2. This system, and the necessary programmers, will increase profits because of greater efficiency.
3. A new system will allow us to upgrade our existing products, as well as to develop new ones.

Step 4. Prepare handouts

Now you can decide what handouts (if any) would add to your presentation. Three major uses of handouts in a presentation are:

1. To reinforce important information.
2. To summarise action items for the audience to follow up.
3. To supply supporting information you don't want cluttering your visual aids.

Once you have decided what handouts would be beneficial you must then decide when you are going to hand them out. There are three alternatives:

Before the presentation
The main problem with this is that your audience may wish to satisfy their curiosity about the contents of your handout as you are speaking. When people are reading, they are not listening. One way to deal with this is to have the handout in place when the audience enters the room. This will allow them to read it before you begin speaking. In addition, you can explain the handout, satisfying their curiosity about its contents.

During the presentation
This must be used carefully. Handouts during a presentation must be distributed quickly and be relevant to the point you are making. Otherwise they will be a distraction, not an aid.

At the end of the presentation
During the presentation you can inform the audience that they will receive a handout covering such and such points at the end of your presentation. This will avoid their taking unnecessary notes.

Step 5. Develop visual aids
Once your organisational pattern has been established, you need to decide if and where you are going to use visual aids. Guidelines for developing and using visual aids in a presentation are discussed later. For now it is important only that you decide how they will fit into your plan.

For example, the third subpoint under the first major idea in our sample presentation states that the old computer system is costing the company money. This point could be illustrated with a graph, or similar visual display showing the cost of the computer over the past three years versus the savings of a new system during the same time span.

Step 6. Main idea preview review sentence

Have you ever heard the saying:

Tell them what you're going to tell them –
Tell them –
Then tell them what you told them!

In other words, preview and review the main points of your presentation. This is very easily done by using a sentence to present your main idea and another sentence to review it, apart from the introduction and conclusion.

Let's go back to the three main points in our example which were:

We need to update our computer system	More programmers are needed to develop our systems	We must finance development

(Remember our objective is to convince upper management that our department needs a 20 per cent larger budget for the next fiscal year.) The preview sentence is then, *'We need to update our computer system, hire more programmers and finance development for several reasons which I intend to discuss today.'* Before the conclusion you can use a similar sentence to review the main ideas as well (ie *'You have now seen why an updated computer system, adequate staff and budget for new development is a good idea.'*).

> All effective presentations make the pattern of organisation crystal clear to the audience.

Step 7. Develop the introduction

You are now ready to develop your introduction. Introductions can serve a number of important purposes. These include:

1. To get the audience's attention and make them concentrate on you, the speaker.
2. To provide background information on your subject.
3. To introduce yourself – tell them who you are and why you are qualified to speak on the subject.

Regardless of the purpose, a good introduction is essential. There are various devices that you can use in an introduction, in addition to providing background material to help get the audience's attention. Here are some of the best.

Anecdote

An anecdote is a short story used to help illustrate a point. It is sometimes humorous but not always. An example might be something like this. *'My son came to me the other day and said, "Dad, if you raise my pocket money by £2 I'll mow the lawn twice a week. For another 10 per cent you will get the best looking lawn in the area." In the same way, if we raise salaries for our production workers 10 per cent, we should expect to increase productivity.'*

Humour

Humour is a great way to break the ice. But beware! Humour must be linked to either the speaker, subject, audience or the occasion.

There is nothing worse than a joke used in an introduction that has no connection with the speech (*ie 'Did you hear about the duck who walked into a shop, ordered a lot of items and asked it all to be put on his bill? Well, today I would like to talk about data processing in our organisation.'*). Nothing is more embarrassing than a joke that falls flat.

Rhetorical question

A rhetorical question is a question with an obvious answer, which the speaker does not expect the audience to supply. An example is, *'How many people here want to make more money?'* This device is an excellent way to get the audience's attention.

Shocking statement

A statement such as, *'Last year enough people died in road accidents to fill every seat in Wembley Stadium. This is why I am going to convince you of the necessity to wear seatbelts.'* This type of statement will help capture your audience's attention.

Step 8. Develop the conclusion

Good conclusions always return to material in your introduction. Normally, they should refer to the background material, rhetorical question, anecdote or data that you used in your introduction.

In persuasive presentations you sometimes need a 'call-to-action' statement in your conclusion. Tell your audience what they need to do (ie should they call a section meeting to implement the new solution? Should they give you the budget increase?). Your conclusion should tell them what specific action they need to take, how to take it, and when it must be taken.

> Introductions and conclusions put the head and tail on the body of your presentation. Without them, or with them not fully developed, your presentation is incomplete and this will be obvious to the audience.

Planning and organising your presentation review checklist

(Use this sheet to help prepare your text presentation.)

Plan your presentation:
For my presentation I have:

☐ Developed objectives

☐ Assessed the audience

Organise your presentation:
For this presentation I have:

☐ Brainstormed main ideas

☐ Brainstormed subpoints

☐ Prepared handouts

☐ Planned visual aids

☐ Stated the benefits (in persuasive presentations)

☐ Stated the main ideas

☐ Structured the introduction

☐ Developed the conclusion

CHAPTER 5

Developing and Using Visual Aids

In this section you will learn how to prepare and use visual aids in your speech. Most presentations in the business and professional world involve overhead transparencies, so we will concentrate on using these. However, tips on using flipcharts, 35 mm slides and other media are also covered in this section.

Use visual aids when you need to:

1. Focus the audience's attention.
2. Reinforce your verbal message (but do not repeat it verbatim).
3. Stimulate interest.
4. Illustrate factors that are hard to visualise.

Don't use visual aids to:

1. Impress your audience with excessively detailed tables or graphs.
2. Avoid interaction with your audience.
3. Make more than one main point.
4. Present simple ideas that can be stated verbally.

When constructing visual aids employ the KISS principle – keep it short and simple! Don't overload charts with too much data. When you do, your audience will quickly lose interest, or get lost.

Avoid charts like this one on page 38.

Table of Monthly Social Security Benefits

Average Indexed Monthly Earnings (AIME)	Benefits For Living Workers And Their Dependents					
	Age 65 Retirement Benefit or Disability Benefit (2)	Age 62 Retirement Benefit	Benefits for Dependents		Child or Spouse Caring for Child	Maximum Family Benefit for Disability
			Spouse Not Caring for Child (3)			
			Age 65	Age 62		
400	282	226	141	106	141	340(6)
450	298	239	149	112	149	382(6)
500	314	251	157	118	157	425(6)
550	330	264	165	124	165	467(6)
600	346			130	173	510(6)
650	362				181	544
700	378				189	568
750	394	410			197	592
800	410				205	616
850	42?				213	640
900	44?				221	664
950	458				229	688
1,000	474				237	712
1,100	506				253	760
1,200	538			02	269	808
1,300	570	456	05	214	285	856
1,400	602	482	301	226	301	904
1,500	634	507	317	238	317	952
1,600	666	533	333	250	333	1,000
1,700	683	547	341	256	341	1,025
1,800(7)	698	559	249	262	349	1,048
1,900	713	571	356	267	356	1,070
2,000	728	583	364	273	364	1,093
2,100	743	595	371	278	371	1,115
2,200	758	607	379	284	379	1,138
2,300	773	619	386	290	286	1,160
2,400	788	631	394	295	394	1,183
2,500	803	643	401	301	401	1,205
2,600	818	655	409	307	409	1,228
2,700	833	667	416	312	416	1,250
2,800(8)	848	679	424	318	424	1,273
2,900	863	691	431	323	431	1,295
3,000(9)	878	703	439	329	439	1,318

Simplify the chart and focus audience attention where you want it.

Information content guidelines for number charts

For number charts – use a maximum of 30 numbers per visual aid. One number can have up to five digits – for example, 18,922 counts as one number. Going above this number of digits causes the visual to look too crowded, and the focus becomes lost.

MONTHLY CUMULATIVE TOTALS			
Accepts	Volume	Returns	Amount
179.880	423.3660	967	334.07
128.864	345.7670	860	287.74
34.221	678.4440	733	982.21
129.775	654.9980	1887	658.89
378.664	739.6000	431	295.58
194.775	187.4659	223	295.50
198.856	189.9570	582	377.89
746.599	879.9560	334	867.73
286.675	385.7689	233	286.57
196.999	285.8678	188	296.97
185.868	286.8786	299	185.90
Totals: 2661.176	5058.0692	6737	4869.05

In this case, *only the totals line* is essential – the rest of the information *could be put in a handout.*

MONTHLY CUMULATIVE TOTALS			
Accepts	Volume	Returns	Amount
2661	5058	6737	4869

Crowding your presentations with too many visual aids and/or too much information will reduce their effectiveness.

Information content guidelines for word charts

For word charts – use a maximum of 36 words per visual aid, excluding the title. Try to fit your material into a maximum of six lines, with no more than six words per line. If you need more room, as in the example below, use more lines, but fewer words. There is no need to repeat every word in your presentation. You simply want to reinforce your main ideas to the audience.

HOW TO ORGANISE YOUR PRESENTATION

It is a good idea to start by developing objectives. Once this is done you need to assess the audience thoroughly. You must complete these steps before you separately brainstorm the main points and the subpoints of your presentation. If it's a persuasive presentation, then you also must decide what the benefits are. You then gather factual information and prepare an outline of your presentation. Also prepare any visual aids, handouts and notes you will need. And don't forget to practise!

This chart is more effective when it is set up as follows:

HOW TO ORGANISE YOUR PRESENTATION

1. Develop objectives
2. Assess the audience
3. Brainstorm the main ideas and subpoints
4. Prepare visual aids, handouts and notes
5. State the benefits (in a persuasive presentation)
6. State main ideas in preview and review sentences
7. Develop the introduction and conclusion

Stating information clearly and concisely on your charts makes it easier for the audience to retain information.

Several examples follow of how different types of information can be effectively presented using visual aids.

CHART AND GRAPH SELECTION – TYPES OF CHART

PER CENT – Shows a comparison as a percentage of the whole. Usually uses the pie chart or map chart.

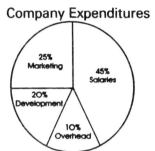

Company Expenditures

PARTS – Shows how items compare or rank. Usually a bar (horizontal lines) or column chart (vertical lines).

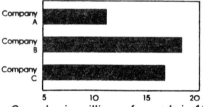

Car sales in millions of pounds in 1987

TIME – Shows changes over a period of time. Column or line charts are most typical.

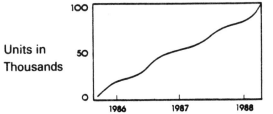

FREQUENCY – Shows the number of items in different numerical ranges. Column and line charts are also used here.

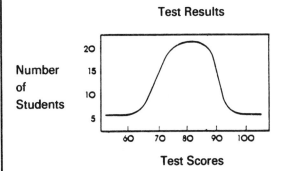

CORRELATION – Shows the relationship between variables. Bar charts and dot charts are used to illustrate correlation.

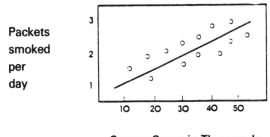

Developing titles for your visual aids

There are three basic titles for your visual aids. Choose the one that best suits your needs:

Subject title. Used when it is not necessary to convey a specific message but only provide information or raw data, as in the example below:

Sales Figures

Thematic title. Used to tell the audience what information they should draw from the data presented. An example would be:

Sales in 1987 were up 22 per cent over 1986

Assertive title. Used when you want to give the audience your opinion about what conclusion they should draw from the data. It is used most often in persuasive presentations, as in the following example:

We should focus our sales effort on the South East

> Concentrate on your audience, not on the methods you are using to attract their attention. Too many presentations rely on other media to carry the message. While external media can certainly help, it's your rapport with the audience that makes the difference between an effective or ineffective presentation.

Using visual aids in your presentation

Case Study 1
John has to give a presentation to his engineering group describing a major new project he is proposing for the company. He has spent weeks preparing for this 30-minute presentation. This project is important to John, and he is very nervous.

John prepared 75 overhead transparencies for the presentation. Each is crammed with information. As the presentation begins John finds that he is spending more time than he thought he would discussing each transparency. His allotted time is running out fast. He speeds up his rate of speech, and to finish on time he shows the last 35 transparencies without any discussion.

Case Study 2
Ian works in a large bank. He must make a presentation on the past, present and future of the bank's corporate finance department to a group of high-ranking departmental managers. Ian is keen for his presentation to go well.

In Ian's 30-minute presentation he will use overhead transparencies, and he has prepared 10 that summarise important information from his written report. Each transparency deals with a single issue, yet has enough information to cover the subject and reinforce the points he is trying to make. He knows that a summary of information on his visual aids will provide enough meat for discussion. Ian's philosophy is to make visual aids work for him, and not let them overwhelm the presentation.

Who do you think was more successful, and why?

_____

_____

_____

_____

Directing the audience's attention
Learn to direct the audience's attention where you want it. When you use visual aids, the audience's attention is divided. To 'win them back' you will need to redirect their focus. This is usually done by switching off the visual aids, and taking a step or two towards the audience.

Tick the technique(s) that you plan to use in your presentations.

I plan to:

_____ Switch off the overhead projector when there is a lengthy explanation about a point in the transparency and there is no need for the audience to watch the screen. (I won't click the machine on and off in a distracting way, but also won't leave it on so long that they focus on the transpaarency and not on me.)

_____ Turn a flipchart page when I have finished referring to it. (If the flipcharts have been prepared in advance, I plan to leave three blank pages between each prepared sheet so my next page won't show until I'm ready for it.)

_____ Erase any writing I have on a blackboard for the reasons outlined above. (Any information noted by the audience and no longer needed for future reference can be erased.)

_____ Break up slide presentations by inserting a black slide at points where an explanation is needed, or when I want to begin another section. This will wake up my audience and help to refocus their attention. I will leave some light on in the room near where I am standing so that I become the focus of attention when the screen goes black.

_____ Show or demonstrate an object by revealing it when it is referred to and then covering it up when it is no longer in use. (If the object is not covered, most people will continue looking out of curiosity and may miss some of my presentation.)

_____ Avoid passing objects around the audience since this is very distracting. (Instead, I will walk into the audience and show the object to everyone briefly, and then make it available at the end of the session.)

> Decide in advance where the audience should focus. Do you want their attention divided between you and the visual aid or do you need their undivided attention?

Figure 1

Positioning of equipment

When using an overhead projector or flipchart, you should add to, not detract from, your presentation. This can be accomplished by placing the overhead screen or flipchart at a 45 degree angle and slightly to one side of the centre of the room. In this way a presenter can occupy the central position and more easily focus the audience's attention on the information being displayed.

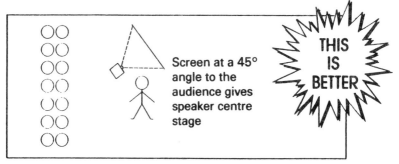

Figure 2

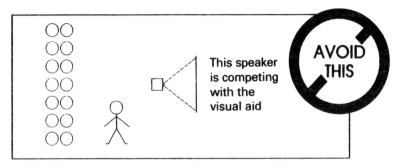

This speaker is competing with the visual aid

AVOID THIS

Figure 3

Figure 2 shows how a room can be set up to maximise audience attention on the speaker. Figure 3 shows the room set up where the speaker is competing for attention with the visual aids.

Where and how to stand

One major problem when using visual aids is that speakers often give their presentation to the screen, and not to the audience. This problem can easily be corrected if the speaker remembers to

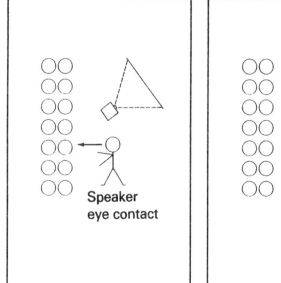

Speaker eye contact

Figure 4

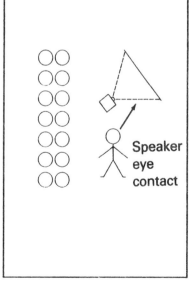

Speaker eye contact

Figure 5

face the audience at all times as illustrated in figure 4. Figure 5 shows what happens when you turn towards the visual aids.

> *Remember:* Don't speak until you have eye contact with your audience! If you must write something on the flipchart, overhead or white board, stop talking while you write.

Tips on using a pointer:

1. Pointers should be used to make a *quick* visual reference on a pictorial chart or to trace the relationship of data on a graph. Pointers are not needed on word charts since you can refer to each point by an item or number.
2. When using a pointer, keep your shoulder facing the audience. Do not hold your arm across your body to refer to something on the screen. Instead, hold the pointer in the hand which is close to the screen.
3. Don't play with the pointer when not using it. Either fold it up and put it away, or put it down.
4. Direct your pointer at the screen, not the overhead projector. Standing at the projector will often block somebody's view of the screen.
5. Leaving the pointer on the overhead projector can focus too much attention on the screen and could detract from the speaker.

Section review: Developing and using visual aids

Tick those items you plan to incorporate in your presentation.

I expect to:

☐ Use the KISS* principle when designing visual aids, and not overload my audience.

☐ Use 'key words' or phrases only for my word charts.

☐ Talk to my audience, not to my visual aids.

☐ Place myself at centre stage.

☐ Use pointers sparingly and not fiddle nervously with them.

---

* Keep it short and simple

CHAPTER 6
Preparing For Your Presentation

In preparing for your presentation you must practise and rehearse as much as possible. This will help you do the very best job you can.

Sometimes a presentation must be prepared at the last minute, leaving little time for preparation and practice. This situation usually leads to increased tension on the part of the speaker and often to a less than professional presentation. Later in this book there are some techniques for organising impromptu or 'on-the-spot' presentations.

How to practise your presentation

A checklist for your practice sessions follows. Staying aware of these steps will help you give a more relaxed, confident and enthusiastic presentation.

_____Make sure your notes are 'key words' only, printed in large letters on index cards. This will provide you with recall cues without having you 'read' to your audience.

_____Mentally run through the presentation to review each idea in sequence.

_____Repeat the above procedure until you become familiar with the flow of ideas and where you plan to use visual aids to support them.

_____ Begin stand-up rehearsals of your presentation. Try to arrange a practice room similar to the one in which you will actually give your presentation.

_____ Give a simulated presentation, idea-for-idea (not word-for-word), using all visual aids. Use your notes as little as possible, and concentrate on the audience.

_____ Practise answers to questions you anticipate from the audience.

_____ Give the full presentation again. If possible, videotape yourself or get a friend to give you some feedback.

_____ Review the videotape and/or the friend's feedback and incorporate any necessary changes.

_____ Give one or two dress rehearsals with the presentation in its final form.

Controlling the presentation environment

Tom worked all week preparing for his quarterly presentation. He has rehearsed (standing up and using his visual aids) and feels prepared and confident. The morning of his presentation he arrived early in order to go over his material for the last time.

As he enters the meeting room for his presentation he notices his manager and his departmental head in the audience. He is nervous but knows he is prepared. He begins his presentation and then moves to the overhead projector to show his first transparency. He flips the switch and nothing happens. He notices the unit is plugged in. He then checks the bulb only to find it's burned out. He knows that most overhead projectors have spare bulbs, but when he looks for it he realises someone didn't bother to replace it. It takes him 20 minutes to track down a new bulb.

This situation could have been avoided if Tom had checked the projector in advance. A few minutes of planning, checking equipment and arranging seating can prevent disasters. Presenters can usually exercise a degree of control over their speaking environment. There are eight items to think about before you speak:

1. *Overhead projectors*
   Make sure that the bulb is not burned out and that there is a spare bulb available. Cleaning the projection screen can sharpen the image. Do you need clear sheets as write-on overlays and pens to use on them?

2. *Flip charts*
   Is there enough paper? Do you have a supply of marking pens available? Have you checked to ensure they have not dried out?

3. *Slide projectors*
   Is it in working condition? Is the lens large enough to project the image size you need? Does your slide holder fit the projector? Is it located so the image will fit the screen? Does it have a remote switch that works, or can you recruit someone to operate it for you? Have you practised using the machine?

4. *Handouts*
   Are handouts easily accessible and in order, so they can be handed out with minimum disruption? Have you arranged for assistance in handing them out if needed?

5. *Pointers*
   Will you need a pointer? Is it within reach, so you can use it when you need it during the presentation?

6. *Microphones*
   If speaking to more than 50–100 people you will probably need a microphone. Before your presentation you may want to request a microphone that allows you to move around. You can request a hand-held mike with a 10–15 foot extension lead

or a mike that will hook on your jacket or tie and allow you to keep your hands free.

7. *Lighting*

Do you need to dim the lights in the room? Check to see if there is a dimmer switch. Some light in the room is desirable in 35 mm slide presentations, so you won't be a voice in the dark. Check to see that all the bulbs and fixtures in the room are working.

8. *Seating arrangement*

If you have control over seating in a room, exercise it. If possible, arrange the seating so that the exit and entrance to the room are at the rear. In this way, if people come and go, it will cause the least amount of distraction.

If you know roughly how many people are going to be present try to control the seating so that there are approximately as many seats as people. This way you won't have your audience sitting in the back of the room.

When you can't practise your presentation – successful impromptu speaking

Jill is invited, along with her manager, to attend a meeting of all departmental heads in the company. She is not expecting to say anything, only to sit and listen. During her manager's presentation, he is asked a question about the department's plans for the coming year. He turns to Jill and says, 'Jill, you've been working on our major project for the past year. Maybe you could say a few words about how this project got started, where it stands and where it is going.'

If something like this happens to you, don't panic! You already know how to organise your thoughts, and you know your job. With these two resources you can respond effectively by taking the following steps:

Think:

Order your thoughts

Any topic can be split up into components. Before you speak break your topic into a pattern such as:

(A) past, present and future (or any time-oriented combination);

(B) topic 1, 2 and 3 (eg production, advertising and marketing);

(C) the pro's and con's of an issue (useful in persuasive situations).

In Jill's case above, the time-ordered sequence fits right in.

Then speak:

Give a few introductory remarks

Before you launch into the meat of your topic give yourself time to get collected. Make some general introductory comments, such as, 'Thanks, I'm pleased to be here today to help provide some information. I didn't plan a formal presentation but would be happy to describe the project we've been working on.'

Develop a clear preview sentence of your main points

You will want to state to yourself and your audience what your key points are. From the example above Jill could simply say, 'I would like to tell you about how we started this project, where it stands and how we plan to develop it'; which is a time ordered sequence.

Deliver the body of the presentation

Talk through each point from your introductory sentence. (In Jill's example: past, present and future). Having an established pattern and knowing where you are going will take some of the stress out of the situation.

If what you are speaking about is controversial, first acknowledge the opposition's case but finish with your own opinion so that you end by summarising your position.

Summarise the main points
Reinforce the main ideas you've touched upon by briefly restating them. Something like, 'In these past few minutes I've tried to give you an overview of how this project began, where it is now and where we think it will go.'

Conclude the presentation
Don't leave your presentation high and dry. End it with a strong, positive, statement. Following our example, 'I hope to attend next month's meeting to report a satisfactory conclusion to our project. I would now be happy to take any questions.'

Section review - prepare for your presentation

1. Rehearse your presentation, standing up and using your visual aids.

2. Control the environment by checking:

   - seating arrangements
   - lighting
   - microphones
   - handouts
   - pointers
   - projection equipment to ensure it is available, in working condition, and has the required back-up supplies

3. When you have to give an impromptu presentation:

   - order your thoughts
   - give a few introductory remarks
   - preview and review the main points
   - end with a strong conclusion

CHAPTER 7
Delivering the Presentation

You must communicate your enthusiasm to the audience if you want them to be enthusiastic about the ideas you present.

Standing stiffly, with little animation in your body, and speaking in a monotone voice without good eye contact is a sure way to deliver a dull speech. We communicate with much more than words. Your non-verbal actions show your feelings. If these channels get cut off because of nerves, your rapport with the audience will suffer.

A great benefit of animated presentation style is that your nervous energy flows outwards. Use a natural, conversational style, and try to relate to people in the audience in a direct and friendly manner. This is vital even in the most formal situations.

You must learn to be aware not only of what you are saying but also how you are saying it! Learn to be your own coach while you are up in front of the audience, checking the items outlined in this section.

Deliver your presentation in the following sequence

1. Introduction.
2. Preview sentence (tell them what you're going to tell them).
3. Main ideas and subpoints (tell them).
4. Benefits (in persuasive presentations).
5. Summary (tell them what you told them).
6. Conclusion.

The following tips will help your presentation become animated and interesting. If you can videotape a rehearsal, watch your delivery. Then rehearse again using some of the techniques described below. Experiment with different presentation styles until you find one that is comfortable and effective.

Posture

Keep your posture erect but relaxed. You want to stand up straight but not stiff. Your feet should be pointed at the audience with your weight evenly distributed. Don't place your weight on one hip, then shift to the other and back again. This shifting can distract the audience.

Movement

Typically, speakers tend to stand in one spot, feet rooted like a tree to the ground. If your presentation will be delivered from a lectern, you should experiment. If appropriate, move to the side or front of the lectern to get nearer to the audience. Many professional speakers do this. It is engaging, and audiences feel more involved. If you are using a microphone, then you may need an extension lead or clip-on mike. (In a formal presentation, or if the lectern is at a head table, this technique may not be practical.)

When not using a lectern, you should normally stay within 4–8 feet of the front row. Don't stay frozen in one spot but don't pace either. An occasional step to either side, or even a half-step towards the audience for emphasis, can enhance your presentation. Stay close, stay direct, and stay involved with your audience.

Gestures

The importance of natural gestures, uninhibited by nerves, cannot be overstated. Too often nervousness restricts this important channel of communication. We use gestures for emphasis in normal conversation without thinking about what we are doing with our hands. *Learn to gesture in front of an audience exactly as you would if you were having an animated conversation with a friend – nothing more, nothing less.*

Using natural gestures won't distract from a presentation; however, doing one of the following certainly will:

- Keeping hands in your pockets

- Or handcuffed behind your back

- Or keeping your arms crossed

- Or in a fig leaf position

- Or wringing your hands nervously

Eye contact

Interviewing someone who looked at the wall or floor when answering your questions would not inspire your confidence in that person. In our culture we expect good, direct eye contact. Yet in many presentations, a speaker will look at a spot on the back of the wall, or at a screen, or at notes – everywhere but into the eyes of the audience.

Eye contact opens the channel of communication between people. It helps to establish and build rapport. It involves the audience in the presentation, and makes the presentations more personal. (This is true even in formal presentations.) Good eye contact between the speaker and audience also helps to relax the speaker by connecting the speaker with the audience and reducing the speaker's feeling of isolation.

The rule of thumb for eye contact is *1–3 seconds per person*. Try not to let your eyes dart around the room. Try to focus on one person, not long enough to make that individual feel uncomfortable, but long enough to pull him or her into your presentation. Then move on to someone else.

When you give a presentation, don't just look at your audience – *see them*. Seek out individuals, and be aware that you are looking at them.

If the group is too large to look at each individual separately, make eye contact with individuals in different parts of the audience. People sitting near the individuals you select will feel that you are actually looking at them. As the distance between a speaker and audience increases, a larger and larger circle of people will feel your 'eye contact'.

Using your voice

There are three main problems associated with voice: a monotone, an inappropriate rate of speech (usually talking too fast) or volume that is too loud or too soft. Make sure your voice is working for you. The following suggestions will help you to speak with a strong, clear voice.

Monotone

Most monotonous voices are caused by anxiety. As the speaker becomes tense, the muscles in the chest and throat become less flexible and air flow is restricted. When this happens, the voice loses its natural animation and becomes monotonous.

To bring back the natural animation you must relax and release tension. Upper and lower body movement are vital. This doesn't have to be dramatic movement – just enough to loosen the muscles and get you to breathe normally. Videotaping, or audio taping, or feedback from a friend, will let you know how you're doing.

Learn to listen to yourself; stay aware not only of what you are saying but also how you are saying it.

Talking too fast

Our average conversational rate of speech is about 125 words per minute. When we become anxious, that rate usually increases. An increased rate of speech is not necessarily a problem if your articulation is good. However, if you are delivering a technical presentation, or one in which the audience needs to take notes, you need to watch your pace.

Another indication that you are talking too fast is when you trip over words. When this happens, slow down. Listen for yourself to say the last word of a sentence, pause where the full stop would be, and then proceed to your next sentence. Pausing during a presentation can be an effective device to allow your important points to sink in. Don't be afraid to allow periods of silence during your presentations. The audience needs time to digest what you are saying.

Problems with volume

In most cases, problems with volume can be solved with practice. You need to stay aware of your volume. It is appropriate to ask during an actual presentation, 'Can you hear me at the back?' The audience will usually be honest because they want to hear what you are saying!

To find out if you have a volume problem before a presentation, ask someone who will give you a straight answer. Ask that person if you can be heard at the back of a room, if you trail off at the end of a sentence, if a lack of volume makes you sound insecure or if you are speaking too loudly.

If your problem is a soft voice, there is a simple exercise to learn how to increase your volume. Recruit two friends to help you. Go into a room that is at least twice the size of the one where you normally give presentations. Have one person sit in the front row, and the other stand against the back wall. Start speaking, and have the person in the back give you a signal when you can be heard clearly. Note your volume level. Check with the person in the front row to make sure you weren't too loud.

A voice consistently too loud sometimes indicates a slight hearing loss. (If your voice is judged too loud you may wish to check with your doctor.) If you are OK, then do the above exercise again, but this time let the person in the front row give you a signal to soften your voice, and then check with the person in the back to make sure you can be heard.

Question-and-answer techniques

How to encourage your audience to ask questions

Often you will want your audience to ask questions. When you have delivered technical information, complicated ideas, or are leading a training session, it is a good idea to check audience comprehension by taking questions.

If you ask for questions passively you won't encourage a response. It's mostly a matter of body language. Standing away from the audience, hands stuffed in your pockets, and mumbling, 'Any questions?' does not encourage questions from an audience.

Those who actively seek questions will step towards the audience, raise a hand and ask, 'Does anyone have questions for me?' You might also ask, 'What questions do you have?' You *assume* the audience will ask questions, and they often do. Also, pause long enough after asking for questions, so the audience will have time to think of questions (the silence should get to them before it gets to you!) Raising your hand will accomplish two things. One, it is the visual signal for questions and will encourage those who might be shy. Also, it helps keep order. The audience will follow your lead and raise their hands, instead of calling out their questions.

How to listen to questions

Perhaps you have seen a speaker listen to a question while pacing back and forth, not look at the questioner, and then interrupt with something like, 'You don't have to finish, I know what you're asking.' The speaker may not know what is being asked until the question is finished. It is important to wait until the questioner has finished.

While the question is being asked you should watch the person who is asking it. It is often possible to pick up clues to the intensity of the question and the feelings behind it and any hidden agendas, if you are aware of body language.

Be careful what you do with your hands during questions. Imagine giving a presentation enthusiastically, and presenting your ideas confidently. Then imagine that when you receive a question, you stand looking at the floor rubbing your hands together nervously. This behaviour can negate the confident image you projected during the presentation. Your hands should stay in a neutral position, arms at your sides, fingers open. Concentrate on the question and listen carefully.

How to answer questions

Prepare for questions
You should be able to anticipate most of the questions you receive. Practise answering them. Prepare for the worst and everything else will seem easier. Some speakers prepare back-up visual aids, to be used only when answering anticipated questions.

Repeat the question
If there is any chance that anyone in the audience didn't hear a question, repeat it for the whole audience. Or, if you get a complicated, emotional or multi-part question, restate it to make sure you understand it. Since we think approximately five times

faster than we speak, repeating the question may give you a few extra seconds to formulate a good answer, too.

Maintain your style

When answering questions, it is important to maintain the same style and demeanour you used in the presentation. A change in demeanour can suggest that you are not confident about your position. When you're asked a question to which you don't know the answer, you don't have to say, 'Sorry, I don't know the answer to that.' Instead you can say, 'I don't know, but I'll find out and get back to you later.'

Involve the whole audience in your answer

Have you seen speakers who get involved with the person who has asked a question and ignore the rest of the audience? In some situations the questioner may try to 'hook' the speaker with a difficult question. You can always tell if a speaker is 'hooked' because he or she is only aware of the person who asked the question.

Employ the 25–75 per cent rule

Direct approximately 25 per cent of your eye contact to the person who asked the question and approximately 75 per cent to the rest of the audience. (This is especially important in a hostile question and answer situation.) Don't ignore the person who asked the question, but don't ignore the rest of the audience either. This will help you stay in command of the situation and keep the audience involved in your presentation.

Don't preface your answer

Sometimes, when we hear a speaker start an answer with, 'That's a very good question; I'm glad you asked it', it may be a sign that the speaker is unsure of the answer.

It's best not to preface answers but simply to go into the answer (after repeating the question, if appropriate). At the end of your question-and-answer session you might say something like, 'Thank you for all your excellent questions.'

Most presentations include time for questions and answers. Sometimes questions are asked during the session and sometimes at the end. In many cases a speaker has the option of where he or she would like to have questions asked. If this is the case, then you can ask the audience to interrupt you whenever they have questions, or you can request that they save their questions until you've finished the presentation.

Final Review Checklist

Delivering your presentation

I plan to:

☐ Stay aware of not only what is said, but how I say it

☐ Be animated, enthusiastic and direct in my delivery

☐ Use eye contact to make my presentation personal and conversational

☐ Keep a clear, strong voice and not speak too fast

Question-and-answer techniques

I plan to:

☐ Ask for questions by stepping forward with my hand raised

☐ Anticipate questions and practise the answers

☐ Watch the questioner and listen carefully to the question

☐ Keep my hands in a neutral position when listening to questions

☐ Repeat the question to make sure everyone heard it, or for clarification

☐ Keep the same style and demeanour that I had during the presentation

☐ Use eye contact and involve the whole audience in my answer

Tick the following items as you prepare and then deliver your presentation.

To deal with anxiety

I plan to:

☐ Breathe deeply

☐ Focus on relaxing

☐ Release tension by unobtrusive isometric exercises

☐ Move during the presentation

☐ Maintain good eye contact with the audience

To plan and organise your presentation

I will:

☐ Develop objectives

☐ Analyse my audience

☐ Brainstorm main ideas

☐ Brainstorm subpoints

☐ Plan handouts

☐ Plan visual aids

☐ State the benefits

☐ Incorporate a main idea, preview, and review sentence

☐ Structure my introduction

☐ Develop a strong conclusion

To develop and use visual aids

I expect to:

☐ Use the KISS principle

☐ Choose the correct type of chart

☐ Use appropriate titles

☐ Refrain from talking to the visual aids

☐ Place myself at centre stage

☐ Use my pointer sparingly

To prepare for the presentation

I will:

☐ Rehearse standing up and using visual aids

☐ Check seating, the audio-visual equipment, all handouts etc

While delivering my presentation

I plan to:

☐ Stay aware of what I'm saying and how I say it

☐ Be animated, enthusiastic and direct

☐ Make my presentation personal and conversational

☐ Use a clear, strong voice

For question-and-answer sessions

I plan to:

☐ Raise my hand and step towards the audience

☐ Watch and listen to the questioner

☐ Repeat the question if necessary

☐ Maintain my style and demeanour

☐ Answer the whole audience with my eye contact

Further Reading from Kogan Page

The Business Guide to Effective Speaking, Jacqueline Dunckel and Elizabeth Parnham, 1985

The Business Guide to Effective Writing, J A Fletcher and D F Gowing, 1987

How to Improve Your Presentation Skills: A Complete Action Kit, Michael Stevens, 1987

How to Make Meetings Work, Malcolm Peel, 1988

How to Organise Effective Conferences and Meetings, 3rd edn, David Seekings, 1987

Never Take No For an Answer: A Guide to Successful Negotiation, Samfrits Le Poole, 1987